AI FOR

TRADING

A simple Guide to Trade Easily with the Power of
Artificial Intelligence (Hidden Trade Secrets Revealed
for Smart Traders)

Nathan G. Carter

TABLE OF CONTENT

Ai for Trading

Introduction

rtificial Intelligence (AI) has revolutionized a number of industries, and trading is no exception. The introduction of artificial intelligence (AI) into the financial markets has transformed trade over the past ten years, bringing with it new opportunities, efficiency, and difficulties. Traders who have embraced artificial intelligence (AI) technologies have seen firsthand how potent algorithms can scan enormous volumes of data, spot trends, and execute trades at speeds and accuracy that are unmatched by humans. With the purpose of guiding you through the world of AI-powered trading, this book provides you with insights into how to use these cutting-edge technologies to improve your trading tactics and financial results.

The financial markets are intrinsically complicated and are influenced by a wide range of factors, such as investor sentiment, geopolitical developments, and economic statistics. Historically, traders have made decisions by combining technical analysis, fundamental analysis, and intuition. But given the amount of data available today, it is practically hard for one person to manually process and analyze all of the pertinent data. AI can help in this situation. Artificial intelligence (AI) can handle and analyze enormous datasets in real-time, spotting patterns and trends that would be impossible for a human to see by using complex models and machine learning techniques. AI-powered trading systems can therefore execute deals more quickly, make better decisions, and adjust to shifting market conditions.

AI's capacity to exclude emotion from decision-making is a major factor in its rise to popularity in trading. Human traders are frequently impacted by emotions that can impair their judgment, such as fear and greed. This emotional component may cause people to make illogical choices, including holding onto losing positions for extended periods of time or selling winning trades too soon. AI, however, is completely impartial. It makes sure that judgments are made on the basis of information and analysis rather than feelings by adhering to a set of predetermined rules and algorithms. In the end, this impartiality can lead to more consistent and successful results by assisting traders in upholding discipline and adhering to their strategy.

AI's capacity to learn and change over time is a key benefit for traders. A kind of artificial intelligence called machine learning allows computers to get better at what they do as more data is fed into them. This means that AI systems can continuously improve their trading methods depending on past performance and current market conditions. For instance, if a specific trading technique has proven effective in the past, the AI system can pinpoint the elements that made that possible and employ those same strategies going forward. On the other hand, if a strategy has continuously underperformed, the AI can modify its methodology to prevent repeating the same errors. AI has a major advantage over conventional trading techniques, which frequently rely on rigid rules and presumptions, because of its capacity to learn and adapt.

AI has not only made decision-making and adaptability better, but it has also completely changed trade execution speed. One of the best examples of how automation and artificial intelligence have changed the trading industry is high-frequency trading, or HFT. HFT entails the use of algorithms to quickly execute a large number of trades in order to profit from tiny price differences that are frequently invisible to human traders. HFT systems can evaluate market circumstances, spot opportunities, and execute trades quickly by utilizing AI. This allows them to frequently outperform other market participants. Although HFT is usually linked with institutional trading, individual traders might gain a competitive advantage by applying the fundamental concepts of speed and efficiency to retail trading as well.

AI has several benefits, but it also has drawbacks. The

possibility for over-reliance on models and algorithms is one of the biggest worries. Even while AI systems are very strong, they are not perfect. They are only as good as the algorithms they are based on and the data they are trained on. AI-driven trading techniques have occasionally resulted in major market disruptions. One such instance is the 2010 "flash crash," which was created by an algorithmic trading program that precipitated a sharp and sudden decline in the U.S. stock market. These incidents serve as a reminder that although AI can improve trading tactics, care must be taken when implementing it and that some degree of human supervision must always be present.

The accessibility of these technology is another issue with AI in trading. Although sophisticated AI systems can be developed and used by huge financial organizations and hedge funds, it might be more difficult for individual traders to obtain the same degree of technology. But things are starting to shift, with more trading platforms driven by AI becoming accessible to regular traders. These platforms make it possible for traders to employ AI without requiring a high level of technical expertise by providing pre-built algorithms and user-friendly interfaces. These technologies will probably become even more available as AI develops, leveling the playing field for individual traders.

It is crucial to realize that artificial intelligence (AI) is not a panacea as we delve deeper into the realm of trading AI. Even while it has many benefits, it is not a surefire way to success. AI-based strategies need to be carefully planned, tested, and risk managed, just like any other trading strategy. It is imperative to approach AI with an attitude of ongoing learning and development. Because of the volatility of the financial markets, what works now could not work tomorrow. AI can assist you in staying ahead of the curve, but it needs to be continuously improved and adjusted.

We will explore the many facets of AI-powered trading in this book, from comprehending the basic ideas behind AI and machine learning to looking at real-world applications in the financial markets. We will go over how to create and backtest AI-driven strategies, how to start using AI trading platforms, and how to combine AI with conventional trading methods. We'll also look at actual case studies of profitable AI traders and potential developments influencing the nexus between AI and finance.

Chapter One

The Basics of Artificial Intelligence and Machine Learning in Trading

Artificial Intelligence (AI) and Machine Learning (ML) are at the forefront of a technological revolution that is transforming industries across the globe, and trading is no exception. The financial markets, which have historically been controlled by human experience and intuition, are becoming into a battlefield for AI-driven tactics. This chapter will cover the basic ideas of artificial intelligence (AI) and machine learning (ML), as well as how and why these technologies are changing the trading business.

Understanding AI and ML Concepts

Fundamentally, artificial intelligence is the creation of computer systems that can carry out operations that often call for human intelligence. Problem-solving, pattern recognition, language comprehension, and decision-making are some of these tasks. AI systems can do complicated tasks on their own because they are made to resemble human cognitive processes.

The study of algorithms and statistical models that let computers learn from and make judgments based on data is known as machine learning, a subset of artificial intelligence. ML systems find patterns and relationships in data, as opposed to traditional programming, which explicitly codes rules and logic. This enables them to make predictions or judgments without explicitly programming for every eventuality that could arise. Because of its capacity for learning and adaptation, machine learning is especially effective in dynamic contexts like the financial markets.

Machine learning algorithms can be used in trading to evaluate historical data, spot trends, and forecast future changes in the market. For instance, an ML algorithm may examine historical stock price fluctuations and identify patterns, like a run of successive uptrends that frequently anticipate a decline in price. After that, the computer can forecast that the stock's value will likely drop and execute a trade in line with that prediction. The algorithm improves its accuracy over time by honing its predictions in light of fresh information.

Types of ML Learning

There are several types of ML algorithms used in trading such as:

Supervised Learning: In supervised learning, the algorithm is trained on a labeled dataset, where the correct answers (such as the direction of a stock's price movement) are provided. The algorithm learns the relationship between the input data and the output labels, allowing it to make predictions on new, unseen data. Common supervised learning techniques include regression, decision trees, and support vector machines.

Unsupervised Learning: Unlike supervised learning, unsupervised learning algorithms work with unlabeled data. The goal is to identify hidden patterns or structures within the data. For example, an unsupervised algorithm might cluster stocks with similar price movements or detect anomalies that could indicate unusual trading activity. Clustering and anomaly detection are common techniques in unsupervised learning.

Reinforcement Learning: In reinforcement learning, the algorithm learns by interacting with its environment and receiving feedback in the form of rewards or penalties. This approach is particularly useful in trading, where the algorithm can continuously learn from the outcomes of its trades. For example, an algorithm might be rewarded for making profitable trades and penalized for losing trades, guiding it to optimize its strategy over time.

Deep Learning: A subset of ML, deep learning involves the use of artificial neural networks with multiple layers (hence "deep") to model complex patterns in data. Deep learning is particularly effective at processing large and complex datasets, such as those found in financial markets. For example, deep learning algorithms can analyze vast amounts of market data, news articles, and social media sentiment to predict price movements.

Why AI is Transforming the Trading Industry?

The trading industry has always been driven by data, analysis, and decision-making. However, the sheer volume of data generated by today's financial markets has made it increasingly difficult for human traders to keep up. This is where AI steps in, offering a range of advantages that are transforming the industry.

Speed and Efficiency: One of the most significant advantages of AI in trading is its speed. AI algorithms can analyze data and execute trades in milliseconds, far faster than any human trader. This speed is particularly crucial in high-frequency trading (HFT), where algorithms capitalize on small price discrepancies across different markets. AI-driven HFT systems can execute thousands of trades in a fraction of a second, profiting from tiny price differences that would be impossible for a human to detect and act upon.

Data-Driven Decision Making: Traditional trading strategies often rely on human intuition and experience. While these factors are valuable, they are also subject to biases and emotions. AI, on the other hand, bases its decisions purely on data and statistical analysis. By eliminating emotional biases, AI can make more objective and consistent trading decisions. For example, an AI system can analyze a wide range of data sources, including historical prices, economic indicators, and market sentiment, to make informed trading decisions.

Ability to Process Vast Amounts of Data: The modern financial market is inundated with data, from price movements and trading volumes to news articles and social media posts. Analyzing this data manually is virtually impossible. AI excels at processing vast amounts of data quickly and efficiently. For example, natural language processing (NLP) algorithms can analyze news articles and social media posts to gauge market sentiment, while ML algorithms can sift through historical price data to identify patterns and trends.

Adaptability and Learning: One of the most powerful aspects of AI is its ability to learn and adapt over time.

Unlike traditional trading strategies, which may become outdated as market conditions change, AI systems continuously learn from new data and refine their strategies. For example, a supervised learning algorithm can be retrained regularly with new market data, allowing it to stay relevant in evolving market conditions. Similarly, a reinforcement learning algorithm can adjust its strategy based on the success or failure of previous trades, improving its performance over time.

Risk Management: AI can also play a critical role in managing risk. By analyzing historical data and real-time market conditions, AI systems can identify potential risks and adjust trading strategies accordingly. For example, an AI algorithm might detect that a stock is becoming increasingly volatile and reduce exposure to that stock to mitigate risk. Additionally, AI can automate stop-loss orders and other risk management tools, ensuring that trades are executed even when the trader is not actively monitoring the market.

Customization and Personalization: AI allows traders to create highly customized trading strategies tailored to their specific goals and risk tolerance. For example, a trader interested in long-term investments can use AI to identify stocks with strong growth potential, while a day trader can use AI to identify short-term price movements.

Additionally, AI-powered trading platforms often allow users to create and backtest their own algorithms, providing a level of personalization that was previously unavailable to individual traders.

Scalability: AI-driven trading systems can easily scale to handle large portfolios and multiple markets simultaneously. This scalability is particularly advantageous for institutional investors and hedge funds, which manage large amounts of capital across various asset classes. For example, an AI system can monitor and trade multiple stocks, bonds, and commodities simultaneously, ensuring that opportunities are not missed due to human limitations.

AI vs. Traditional Trading: AI-driven trading uses cutting-edge algorithms and data processing power to automate and improve the trading process, whereas traditional trading depends on human intuition, expertise, and manual analysis. The transition from human to automated trading signifies more than just increased productivity; it also signifies a fundamental alteration in the way markets function. Artificial intelligence (AI) processes information at a speed and scale that is unmatched by humans, enabling more rapid and accurate trading decisions. AI also has a significant edge over traditional trading strategies, which could eventually become outdated or ineffective because they can't learn from data and adjust

17

to changing market conditions.

Although artificial intelligence (AI) offers numerous advantages for trading, it's critical to realize that there isn't a single, universally applicable solution. Successful AI trading requires a deep understanding of the technology, careful strategy design, constant monitoring, and tweaking. AI can help you become a better trader, but it cannot replace sound trading tactics and disciplined risk management.

As we go deeper into AI and ML in trading throughout the book, you will have a better understanding of these subjects. Additionally, you will discover how to use these technologies to improve your trading performance. From understanding the foundations of AI and ML to developing and implementing your own AI-driven strategies, this book will provide you the knowledge and abilities you need to succeed in the rapidly evolving field of AI-powered trading.

Chapter Two

Getting Started with AI-Powered Trading Platforms

The adoption of Artificial Intelligence in trading has surged in recent years, with traders and investors seeking to harness the power of algorithms and data to gain a competitive edge. To leverage AI effectively in your trading, the first step is to choose the right platform. In this chapter, we'll explore some of the most popular AI trading platforms, discuss the features that make them stand out, and guide you through the process of setting up your AI trading account.

Popular AI Trading Platforms

The rise of AI in trading has led to the development of various platforms that cater to different types of traders, from beginners to seasoned professionals. These platforms offer a range of features, including automated trading systems, advanced analytics, and customizable algorithms. Below are some of the best AI trading platforms available today:

MetaTrader 4 and 5 (MT4/MT5):

Although not AI-specific, MetaTrader is one of the most popular platforms for retail traders due to its flexibility and extensive library of custom indicators and expert advisors (EAs). EAs are scripts that automate trading strategies, and with the right coding, they can incorporate AI and machine learning models.

Ideal for: Traders looking for a customizable platform with a strong community and a wide range of tools.
Features: Algorithmic trading, backtesting, real-time data analysis, and integration with various brokers.

TradeStation:

TradeStation is a powerful trading platform that offers a suite of tools for AI-driven trading. With its easy-to-use development environment, traders can create and backtest their AI algorithms. TradeStation also supports automated trading strategies, making it a popular choice for traders who want to integrate AI into their trading routines.

Ideal for: Experienced traders and developers interested in creating their own AI-based trading strategies.

Features: AI-driven analysis, automated trading, backtesting, customizable algorithms, and access to a large data library.

QuantConnect:

QuantConnect is a cloud-based platform that allows traders to build, test, and deploy AI trading algorithms. It supports multiple programming languages, including Python and C#, and provides access to extensive historical data for backtesting. QuantConnect is particularly popular among quantitative traders and those with a strong programming background.

Ideal for: Quantitative traders and developers seeking a platform with robust backtesting and algorithm development capabilities.

Features: Cloud-based infrastructure, AI and ML integration, access to historical data, multi-asset trading, and community support.

AlgoTrader:

AlgoTrader is an institutional-grade platform designed for algorithmic trading across various asset classes, including equities, forex, and cryptocurrencies. It integrates AI and machine learning algorithms, enabling traders to automate their strategies and execute trades at high speeds. AlgoTrader is suitable for both retail and institutional traders looking for a comprehensive AI trading solution. Ideal for: Professional traders and institutions requiring advanced AI-driven trading capabilities.

Features: AI integration, automated trading, multi-asset support, high-frequency trading, and API access.

Kavout:

Kavout offers a unique AI-driven trading platform that combines machine learning with traditional quantitative analysis. Its flagship product, the Kai Score, ranks stocks based on AI analysis, helping traders identify investment opportunities. Kavout's platform also allows users to build and test their own AI-powered trading strategies.

Ideal for: Traders and investors seeking AI-driven stock analysis and customizable trading strategies.

Features: AI-powered stock rankings, strategy development, backtesting, and real-time market data.

Numerai:

Numerai is a decentralized hedge fund that crowdsources AI models from data scientists around the world. Traders and developers can submit their AI models, which are then combined to create a collective trading strategy. Numerai is unique in that it rewards contributors based on the performance of their models, making it an exciting platform for data scientists and AI enthusiasts.

Ideal for: Data scientists and AI developers interested in contributing to a collective trading strategy.

Features: Crowdsourced AI models, cryptocurrency rewards, decentralized platform, and collaborative strategy development.

TuringTrader:

TuringTrader is a platform that allows traders to create and deploy AI-powered strategies using Python. The platform provides access to various data sources and supports backtesting, making it an excellent choice for traders with programming skills who want to develop and implement AI-driven strategies.

Ideal for: Python developers and traders looking to build custom AI trading strategies.

Features: Python-based algorithm development, backtesting, real-time execution, and multi-asset support. Each of these platforms offers a unique set of features, so the best one for you will depend on your trading style, level of expertise, and specific needs. Whether you're looking for a user-friendly interface with pre-built AI tools or a customizable platform for developing your own algorithms, there's a platform that can meet your requirements.

Setting Up Your AI Trading Account

Once you've selected the platform that best suits your needs, the next step is to set up your AI trading account. While the exact process may vary depending on the platform, the following steps provide a general guide to getting started.

Create an Account:

The first step is to sign up for an account on your chosen platform. This typically involves providing your personal information, including your name, email address, and contact details. Some platforms may also require you to verify your identity by submitting documents such as a passport or driver's license.

Choose a Brokerage:

Many AI trading platforms are integrated with various brokers. If you're using a platform like MetaTrader, you'll need to select a broker that supports the platform and meets your trading needs. Consider factors such as trading fees, available assets, and customer support when choosing a broker. Some platforms, like QuantConnect, allow you to connect multiple broker accounts, giving you greater flexibility in your trading.

Fund Your Account:

Once you've chosen a broker and created your trading account, you'll need to deposit funds to start trading. Most platforms accept various payment methods, including bank transfers, credit/debit cards, and even cryptocurrencies. Be sure to check the minimum deposit requirements and any fees associated with funding your account.

Download and Install the Trading Software:

Depending on the platform, you may need to download and install trading software on your computer or mobile device. Platforms like MetaTrader and TradeStation require you to install their software, while others, like QuantConnect, are cloud-based and accessible through a web browser. Follow the platform's installation instructions to ensure everything is set up correctly.

Configure Your Trading Settings:

Once your account is funded and your software is installed,

it's time to configure your trading settings. This includes selecting your preferred trading assets, setting your risk tolerance, and configuring any AI algorithms or automated trading systems you plan to use. Some platforms allow you to customize your AI models or select from pre-built strategies. Be sure to test your settings in a demo account if available before going live with real money.

Backtest Your Strategy:

Before you start live trading, it's essential to backtest your AI-driven strategy using historical data. Backtesting allows you to see how your strategy would have performed in the past, helping you identify any potential issues or areas for improvement. Most AI trading platforms offer built-in backtesting tools that allow you to simulate your strategy across different market conditions.

Go Live:

After backtesting and refining your strategy, you're ready to go live. Start by trading with a small amount of capital to minimize risk while you get comfortable with the platform and your AI system. Monitor your trades closely and make adjustments as needed. As you gain confidence in your strategy, you can gradually increase your trading capital.
Monitor and Adjust:

AI trading is not a "set it and forget it" approach. While AI can automate many aspects of trading, it's crucial to monitor your system regularly and make adjustments as needed. Markets are dynamic, and your AI strategy may need to be updated to reflect new data or changing conditions. Most platforms provide real-time performance tracking and analytics tools to help you stay on top of your trades.

Continuously Learn and Improve:

AI and machine learning are constantly evolving fields, and the best traders are those who continuously learn and improve. Stay up to date with the latest developments in AI trading, and don't be afraid to experiment with new strategies or algorithms. Many platforms offer educational resources, forums, and communities where you can connect with other traders and developers.

Setting up your AI trading account is just the beginning of your journey into the world of AI-powered trading. By choosing the right platform, configuring your settings, and continuously monitoring and refining your strategies, you can harness the power of AI to enhance your trading performance and achieve your financial goals.

Chapter Three

Leveraging AI for Predictive Analytics

In the ever-evolving world of financial markets, predicting future trends and price movements is the key to profitable trading. Traditional methods, such as technical and fundamental analysis, have long been the go-to strategies for traders. However, with the advent of Artificial Intelligence (AI), a new era of predictive analytics is emerging, offering more accurate, data-driven insights. In this chapter, we will explore how AI predicts market trends and how it can be integrated with technical and fundamental analysis to enhance your trading strategies.

How AI Predicts Market Trends

Predictive analytics is a crucial aspect of AI-powered trading. At its core, predictive analytics involves using data, statistical algorithms, and machine learning techniques to identify the likelihood of future outcomes based on historical data. In trading, this means forecasting market trends, price movements, and potential investment opportunities.

AI excels at predictive analytics because of its ability to

process vast amounts of data quickly and identify complex patterns that may not be visible to human traders. Here's how AI predicts market trends:

Data Collection and Processing:

AI-driven predictive analytics starts with data collection. Financial markets generate an enormous amount of data every day, including price movements, trading volumes, news reports, economic indicators, and even social media sentiment. AI systems can gather and process this data in real-time, providing traders with up-to-date information that is critical for making informed decisions.

Advanced AI models can also process unstructured data, such as news articles and tweets, using Natural Language Processing (NLP) to gauge market sentiment and predict how it might affect prices. By analyzing both structured and unstructured data, AI provides a more comprehensive view of the market.

Pattern Recognition:

Once the data is collected and processed, AI algorithms are used to identify patterns that indicate potential market trends. Machine learning models, such as neural networks and decision trees, are particularly effective at recognizing complex patterns in data that traditional statistical methods may miss.

For example, an AI model might identify a pattern where a specific economic indicator consistently leads to a rise or fall in stock prices. By recognizing this pattern, the AI system can predict future price movements when similar conditions arise.

Trend Analysis and Forecasting:

After identifying patterns, AI systems use them to forecast future market trends. This involves predicting the direction of price movements, the potential magnitude of those movements, and the likelihood of specific events, such as a stock reaching a certain price target.

AI models can be trained on historical data to improve their accuracy over time. For instance, a model might be trained to recognize bullish or bearish signals based on past market behavior. As the model processes more data, it becomes better at predicting future trends, making it a valuable tool for traders looking to capitalize on market movements.

Real-Time Adjustments:

One of the significant advantages of AI in predictive analytics is its ability to make real-time adjustments. Markets are dynamic, and conditions can change rapidly. AI systems continuously analyze new data and adjust their predictions accordingly. This real-time analysis allows traders to respond quickly to market changes, improving their chances of making profitable trades.

For example, if an AI system detects a sudden change in market sentiment due to breaking news, it can update its predictions and recommend adjusting your trading strategy to take advantage of the new information.

Scenario Analysis:

AI can also perform scenario analysis, which involves predicting how different market conditions might impact asset prices. This is particularly useful for traders looking to hedge their positions or assess the potential risks and rewards of different trading strategies.

By simulating various scenarios, AI systems can provide insights into how specific events, such as a central bank interest rate decision or geopolitical developments, might affect the market. This allows traders to prepare for different outcomes and make more informed decisions.

Machine Learning Models in Predictive Analytics

Several machine learning models are commonly used in AI-driven predictive analytics. These include:

Time Series Analysis: Time series models, such as ARIMA (Auto-Regressive Integrated Moving Average) and LSTM (Long Short-Term Memory) networks, are used to analyze and forecast time-dependent data, such as stock prices and trading volumes.

Classification Models: Classification algorithms, such as decision trees and random forests, can be used to categorize data and predict the likelihood of specific outcomes, such as whether a stock will move up or down.

Regression Models: Regression models, such as linear regression and support vector regression, are used to predict continuous variables, such as the expected price of a stock at a future date.

Deep Learning Models: Deep learning models, such as convolutional neural networks (CNNs) and recurrent neural networks (RNNs), are particularly effective at processing large datasets and identifying intricate patterns in data.

By leveraging these machine learning models, AI can provide traders with highly accurate predictions, helping them make better-informed decisions and improve their trading performance.

Integrating AI with Technical and Fundamental Analysis

While AI-driven predictive analytics offers powerful insights, it's most effective when combined with traditional trading strategies, such as technical and fundamental analysis. By integrating AI with these approaches, traders can develop more robust and reliable trading strategies.

Technical Analysis with AI:

Technical analysis involves studying historical price charts and using indicators to predict future price movements. Common technical indicators include moving averages, relative strength index (RSI), and Fibonacci retracement levels.

AI enhances technical analysis by automating the process of identifying patterns and signals. For example, AI can scan multiple charts simultaneously and detect patterns such as head and shoulders, double tops, or trend reversals in real-time. This allows traders to act quickly on trading opportunities.

AI can also optimize technical indicators by fine-tuning their parameters based on historical data. For instance, an AI system might adjust the settings of a moving average crossover strategy to maximize its profitability under specific market conditions.

AI-Enhanced Trading Strategies:

AI can be used to develop and implement advanced trading strategies that go beyond traditional technical analysis. For example, AI-driven strategies might combine multiple technical indicators with machine learning models to create a more sophisticated trading algorithm.

These AI-enhanced strategies can be backtested using historical data to evaluate their performance and optimize their parameters. By continuously learning from new data, AI systems can adapt their strategies to changing market conditions, making them more resilient and effective over time.

AI can also automate the execution of these strategies, allowing traders to take advantage of opportunities around the clock without the need for manual intervention.

Fundamental Analysis with AI:

Fundamental analysis involves evaluating the intrinsic value of an asset by analyzing financial statements, economic indicators, and other relevant factors. Traditionally, this process requires significant time and effort, as traders must sift through large amounts of data to make informed decisions.

AI simplifies and enhances fundamental analysis by automating data collection and analysis. For example, AI can analyze earnings reports, balance sheets, and cash flow statements to assess a company's financial health. It can also process macroeconomic data, such as GDP growth, inflation rates, and interest rates, to evaluate the broader economic environment.

Moreover, AI can use sentiment analysis to gauge investor sentiment by analyzing news articles, social media posts, and analyst reports. This allows traders to gain insights into market sentiment and incorporate it into their fundamental analysis.

By integrating AI with fundamental analysis, traders can quickly identify undervalued or overvalued assets and make more informed investment decisions.

Combining Technical and Fundamental Analysis with AI:

Technical and fundamental analysis are frequently used in unison by the most successful traders to guide their trading decisions. AI can provide a thorough examination of both price patterns and underlying fundamentals, bridging the gap between these two methods.

An AI system might, for instance, utilize fundamental analysis to verify that the company's finances support the price movement while concurrently employing technical analysis to spot a possible breakout in the price of a stock. This multifaceted strategy can lower the likelihood of misleading signals and improve prediction accuracy.

AI can also combine technical indications with fundamental data to optimize trade timing. An AI system may suggest purchasing a stock, for example, if its fundamentals show significant growth potential and its technical indicators show a bullish trend.

AI-Based Risk Management:

Managing risk well is essential to successful trading. AI may be extremely helpful in risk management by evaluating possible risks and rewards by evaluating past data and current market conditions.

AI, for instance, may determine the likelihood of certain outcomes based on past volatility and modify your trading approach as necessary. To reduce possible losses, it can also automate position size and stop-loss orders.

By identifying assets with low correlations, AI can assist traders in diversifying their portfolios and lowering overall risk. AI can assist you in more successfully managing risk and safeguarding your cash by continuously analyzing market conditions and modifying your approach.

AI-Driven Portfolio Management

Beyond individual trades, AI can also assist in portfolio management. AI systems can analyze your entire portfolio, assess its risk and return characteristics, and recommend adjustments to optimize its performance.

For example, AI can rebalance your portfolio based on

changing market conditions, ensuring that your asset allocation remains aligned with your investment goals. It can also identify opportunities to diversify your holdings or hedge against potential risks.

By integrating AI with both technical and fundamental analysis, you can develop more sophisticated and effective trading strategies. AI enhances your ability to analyze data, identify trends, and make informed decisions, ultimately improving your trading performance.

As you continue to explore the possibilities of AI in trading, keep in mind that successful trading requires a combination of knowledge, discipline, and adaptability. While AI provides powerful tools for predictive analytics and strategy development, it's essential to continuously monitor your trades, refine your strategies, and stay informed about market developments.

Chapter Four

Designing and Backtesting AI Trading Strategies

In the realm of AI-powered trading, designing and backtesting trading strategies are crucial steps that can significantly influence your trading success. Developing a robust AI trading strategy involves creating algorithms that can analyze data, make predictions, and execute trades. Backtesting, on the other hand, allows you to test these strategies against historical data to evaluate their performance and refine them before live deployment. This chapter will guide you through the process of creating your first AI trading strategy and the best practices for backtesting and optimizing your AI models.

Creating Your First AI Trading Strategy

Designing an AI trading strategy begins with defining your trading goals and determining how AI can be applied to achieve those goals. An effective strategy is one that not only leverages AI for its predictive power but also aligns with your risk tolerance, trading style, and market knowledge.

Define Your Objectives:

Start by clearly outlining your trading objectives. Are you looking to generate short-term gains through high-frequency trading, or are you interested in long-term investments based on fundamental analysis? Your objectives will guide the design of your AI trading strategy and help you choose the appropriate algorithms and data inputs.

For example, if your goal is to capitalize on short-term price movements, your strategy might focus on high-frequency trading and use AI to identify and act on micro-trends. Conversely, if you're aiming for long-term growth, your strategy might incorporate fundamental analysis and use AI to predict broader market trends.

Gather and Prepare Data:

Data is the backbone of any AI trading strategy. Collect relevant data, including historical price data, trading volumes, economic indicators, and market sentiment. The quality and quantity of your data will directly impact the effectiveness of your AI models.

Ensure that your data is clean and well-organized. Data

pre-processing steps, such as handling missing values, normalizing data, and removing outliers, are essential to improve the accuracy of your AI models. Use data sources that are reliable and up-to-date to ensure that your models are trained on relevant information.

Select AI Algorithms:

Choose the AI algorithms that best fit your trading objectives. Commonly used algorithms in trading include machine learning models like linear regression, decision trees, random forests, and deep learning models like neural networks.

For instance, if you want to predict future price movements based on historical data, you might use regression models or recurrent neural networks (RNNs). If your strategy involves classifying market conditions into different categories, decision trees or support vector machines (SVMs) might be suitable.

Develop the Trading Algorithm:

With your data and algorithms in place, it's time to develop your trading algorithm. This involves coding the logic that will drive your trading decisions. Your algorithm should include rules for entering and exiting trades, position sizing, and risk management.

Incorporate features such as trend indicators, momentum signals, and volatility measures into your algorithm. Ensure that your algorithm is designed to handle different market conditions and adjust its behavior based on changing data. Implement Risk Management:

Risk management is a critical component of any trading strategy. Incorporate risk management rules into your AI algorithm to protect your capital and minimize potential losses. This might include setting stop-loss orders, defining maximum drawdown limits, and diversifying your trades. Consider using position sizing techniques to manage risk based on your confidence in the algorithm's predictions. For example, allocate a smaller portion of your capital to trades with higher uncertainty and a larger portion to trades with higher confidence.

Test and Validate the Strategy:

Before deploying your AI trading strategy, it's essential to test and validate its performance using historical data. This helps you identify any issues with the algorithm and ensures that it behaves as expected under different market conditions.

Perform walk-forward testing to evaluate how the strategy performs on data that was not used during the development phase. This helps assess the strategy's robustness and adaptability to new data.

Backtesting and Optimizing Your AI Models

Backtesting is a crucial step in evaluating the performance of your AI trading strategy. It involves testing the strategy against historical data to assess its effectiveness and identify areas for improvement. Optimization involves refining the strategy to enhance its performance and adaptability.

Conducting Backtests:

Backtesting involves applying your AI trading strategy to historical data to evaluate its performance. This process helps you understand how the strategy would have performed in the past and provides insights into its potential effectiveness.

Use historical data that covers a range of market conditions, including bull and bear markets, to ensure that your backtests are comprehensive. This will help you identify how the strategy performs in different scenarios and assess its robustness.

Analyze key performance metrics, such as return on investment (ROI), Sharpe ratio, maximum drawdown, and win-to-loss ratio. These metrics provide insights into the strategy's profitability, risk-adjusted returns, and overall performance.

Overfitting:

Overfitting occurs when a trading strategy performs exceptionally well on historical data but fails to generalize to new, unseen data. This can result from excessive optimization or including too many variables in the model.

To avoid overfitting, use techniques such as cross-validation and out-of-sample testing. Cross-validation involves dividing your data into multiple subsets and testing the strategy on different subsets to ensure that it performs consistently. Out-of-sample testing involves evaluating the strategy on data that was not used during the development phase.

Optimize AI Models:

Optimization involves refining your AI trading strategy to enhance its performance. This might include adjusting algorithm parameters, incorporating additional features, or modifying trading rules.

Use optimization techniques such as grid search, random search, or evolutionary algorithms to find the best parameters for your model. Grid search involves systematically testing different combinations of parameters, while random search involves sampling random combinations. Evolutionary algorithms use techniques inspired by natural evolution to find optimal solutions.

Ensure that your optimization process is robust and does not lead to overfitting. Validate the optimized strategy using out-of-sample data to confirm that it performs well under different conditions.

Implementing Real-Time Testing:

After backtesting and optimizing your AI trading strategy, consider implementing real-time testing using a demo account or paper trading environment. This allows you to test the strategy in live market conditions without risking real capital.

Real-time testing helps you identify any issues with the algorithm's execution and ensures that it operates as expected in real-world scenarios. Monitor the strategy's performance and make adjustments as needed based on real-time feedback.

Continuous Improvement:

AI trading strategies should be continuously monitored and improved. As market conditions change and new data becomes available, regularly update and refine your strategy to maintain its effectiveness.

Implement a feedback loop that allows you to evaluate the strategy's performance, identify areas for improvement, and make adjustments based on new insights and data.

Documentation and Reporting:

Document the development, backtesting, and optimization processes of your AI trading strategy. Keep detailed records of the data used, algorithm parameters, performance metrics, and any modifications made to the strategy.

Regularly generate reports to track the strategy's performance and assess its effectiveness. These reports can help you make data-driven decisions and ensure that your strategy remains aligned with your trading objectives.

Designing and backtesting AI trading strategies require a combination of technical skills, market knowledge, and rigorous testing. By following best practices and leveraging AI's predictive power, you can develop robust trading strategies that enhance your trading performance and help you achieve your financial goals. Remember to continuously monitor and refine your strategies to adapt to changing market conditions and maintain a competitive edge.

Chapter Five

Risk Management with AI in Trading

Risk management is a cornerstone of successful trading. In an environment where market conditions can shift rapidly and unpredictably, safeguarding your capital and managing potential losses are critical to long-term profitability. Artificial Intelligence (AI) is revolutionizing how traders approach risk management by providing advanced tools and techniques to better anticipate, mitigate, and manage risks. This chapter explores how AI helps mitigate trading risks and how it can be used to automate stop-loss and take-profit strategies.

How AI Helps Mitigate Trading Risks

AI's ability to process vast amounts of data and identify complex patterns makes it an invaluable tool for managing trading risks. By leveraging AI, traders can gain deeper insights into market conditions, enhance their risk management strategies, and reduce the likelihood of significant losses. Here's how AI contributes to risk management in trading:

Predictive Risk Analysis

AI models can analyze historical data and identify patterns that signal potential risks. For example, machine learning algorithms can detect changes in market volatility, liquidity, and trading volumes that might indicate heightened risk.

By forecasting potential risk events based on historical trends, AI can provide early warnings and help traders adjust their strategies to mitigate potential losses. This predictive capability enables proactive risk management rather than reactive measures.

Real-Time Risk Assessment:

One of AI's most significant advantages is its ability to analyze data in real-time. AI systems can continuously monitor market conditions, news events, and economic indicators to assess current risk levels.

Real-time risk assessment allows traders to respond quickly to changing market conditions. For instance, if AI detects an increase in volatility or adverse news affecting a specific asset, it can alert traders to adjust their positions or implement protective measures.

Risk Modeling and Scenario Analysis:

AI can create sophisticated risk models that simulate different market scenarios and assess their potential impact on trading positions. This scenario analysis helps traders understand how various factors, such as interest rate changes or geopolitical events, might affect their portfolios. By modeling different scenarios, AI can provide insights into potential risks and help traders develop contingency plans. This proactive approach enables better preparedness and reduces the likelihood of unexpected losses.

Enhanced Data Analysis:

Traditional risk management often relies on historical data and simple metrics. AI, however, can analyze vast amounts of structured and unstructured data, including price movements, economic reports, and social media sentiment. AI's ability to process and analyze diverse data sources provides a more comprehensive view of market risks. For example, sentiment analysis using Natural Language Processing (NLP) can gauge investor sentiment and its potential impact on market stability.

Risk Diversification and Portfolio Management:

AI can assist in diversifying trading portfolios by analyzing correlations between different assets and recommending optimal asset allocations. This helps reduce risk by spreading investments across assets that are less likely to move in tandem.

AI-driven portfolio management can automatically adjust asset allocations based on changing risk profiles and market conditions. This dynamic approach to portfolio management enhances risk control and maximizes returns. Anomaly Detection:

AI systems can detect anomalies or unusual patterns in trading data that might signal potential risks. For example, if AI identifies an unexpected surge in trading volume or price fluctuations, it can alert traders to investigate further. Anomaly detection helps identify potential issues early, allowing traders to take corrective actions before they escalate into significant problems.

Behavioral Analysis:

AI can analyze trader behavior and identify patterns that might indicate risky trading practices. For example, if AI detects frequent high-risk trades or deviations from established trading rules, it can provide feedback and recommend adjustments.

By monitoring trading behavior and providing insights into potential risks, AI can help traders improve their decision-making and adhere to sound risk management practices.
Using AI to Automate Stop-Loss and Take-Profit

Automating risk management processes, such as stop-loss and take-profit orders, is another area where AI excels. These automated mechanisms help protect trading capital and lock in profits by executing trades based on predefined conditions. Here's how AI enhances stop-loss and take-profit automation:

AI Stop-Loss Automation:

Stop-loss orders are designed to limit potential losses by automatically closing a position when the price reaches a specified level. AI can enhance stop-loss automation by dynamically adjusting stop-loss levels based on real-time market conditions.

For example, AI systems can analyze market volatility and adjust stop-loss levels to account for sudden price movements. This ensures that stop-loss orders are effective in protecting capital without being triggered by normal market fluctuations.

Dynamic Stop-Loss Adjustment:

AI can continuously monitor market conditions and adjust stop-loss levels in real-time. For instance, if AI detects increased volatility or a shift in market trends, it can modify stop-loss levels to reflect the new risk profile.

Dynamic adjustment of stop-loss levels helps prevent premature execution of stop-loss orders and ensures that they are aligned with current market conditions.

AI Take-Profit Automation:

Take-profit orders are used to lock in profits by automatically closing a position when the price reaches a predetermined level. AI can enhance take-profit automation by optimizing profit-taking levels based on market trends and historical data.

AI systems can analyze historical price movements and identify optimal take-profit levels that maximize returns while minimizing the risk of price reversals.

Trailing Stop-Loss and Take-Profit:

Trailing stop-loss and take-profit orders are designed to

lock in profits and protect gains by adjusting stop-loss and take-profit levels as the price moves in a favorable direction. AI can automate trailing stop-loss and take-profit orders by continuously updating these levels based on real-time price movements.

For example, if a stock price increases, AI can automatically adjust the trailing stop-loss level to secure gains while allowing for potential further upside.

Risk Management Algorithms:

AI can develop sophisticated algorithms for managing stop-loss and take-profit orders. These algorithms can take into account various factors, such as market volatility, asset correlations, and historical performance, to optimize risk management.

By using AI-driven risk management algorithms, traders can ensure that their stop-loss and take-profit orders are well-calibrated and aligned with their overall trading strategy.

Backtesting and Optimization:

Before deploying automated stop-loss and take-profit

systems, it's essential to backtest and optimize those using historical data. AI can assist in backtesting these automated mechanisms to evaluate their effectiveness and make necessary adjustments.

Backtesting helps identify potential issues and refine the parameters of stop-loss and take-profit orders to ensure they perform well under different market conditions.

Integration with Trading Platforms:

Many AI trading platforms offer built-in features for automating stop-loss and take-profit orders. These platforms can integrate AI algorithms with trading systems to execute orders automatically based on predefined conditions.

Ensure that your AI trading platform supports the automation of stop-loss and take-profit orders and that it provides the flexibility to customize these orders based on your trading preferences.

By leveraging AI for risk management and automating stop-loss and take-profit orders, traders can enhance their ability to protect capital, manage risks, and maximize profits. AI's predictive capabilities, real-time analysis, and automation features provide valuable tools for navigating the complexities of financial markets and achieving trading success.

As you incorporate AI into your risk management strategies, remember to continuously monitor and refine your approach based on real-time performance and market conditions. Effective risk management is an ongoing process that requires vigilance, adaptability, and a commitment to leveraging advanced technologies for optimal results.

Chapter Six

Real-Life Applications of AI in Trading

A rtificial Intelligence (AI) has rapidly evolved from a novel technology to a fundamental tool in trading, influencing how trades are executed and how strategies are developed. This chapter delves into real-life applications of AI in trading, highlighting case studies of successful AI traders and examining how hedge funds and institutional investors are leveraging AI to gain a competitive edge in the financial markets.

Case Studies of Successful AI Traders

The transformative power of AI in trading is evident from numerous success stories in the financial world. These case studies not only illustrate the potential of AI to revolutionize trading strategies but also provide practical insights into how AI can be effectively implemented to achieve substantial profits.

Case Study 1: Renaissance Technologies

Renaissance Technologies, a hedge fund founded by Jim

Simons, is renowned for its use of AI and quantitative models to achieve remarkable trading success. The firm's Medallion Fund, which employs complex algorithms and machine learning techniques, has consistently delivered exceptional returns.

Renaissance Technologies uses AI to analyze vast amounts of market data, identify patterns, and make trading decisions with high precision. The firm's success can be attributed to its ability to integrate advanced data analytics with sophisticated trading strategies, allowing it to capitalize on market inefficiencies and generate substantial profits.

Case Study 2: Two Sigma

Two Sigma Investments is another prominent hedge fund that has embraced AI and machine learning to drive its trading strategies. The firm leverages AI to process large datasets, including financial metrics, social media sentiment, and alternative data sources, to inform its trading decisions. Two Sigma's use of AI has enabled it to develop predictive models that can anticipate market movements and identify profitable trading opportunities. By integrating AI with traditional quantitative methods, Two Sigma has achieved impressive performance and positioned itself as a leader in AI-driven trading.

Case Study 3: Sentient Technologies

Sentient Technologies is a company that has applied AI to develop an advanced trading platform known as Sentient Investment Management. The platform uses evolutionary algorithms and machine learning to optimize trading strategies and adapt to changing market conditions.

Sentient Technologies' approach involves using AI to create and test multiple trading strategies simultaneously, allowing it to identify the most effective ones. This innovative use of AI has enabled the company to achieve competitive returns and gain recognition in the financial industry.

Case Study 4: IBM Watson in Trading

IBM Watson, a leading AI platform, has been applied in the trading industry to enhance decision-making and improve trading outcomes. Watson's natural language processing capabilities allow it to analyze news articles, financial reports, and other textual data to gauge market sentiment and predict price movements.

One notable application of IBM Watson in trading is its use

by financial institutions to analyze macroeconomic trends and identify investment opportunities. By leveraging Watson's AI-powered insights, traders have been able to make more informed decisions and achieve favorable results.

Case Study 5: BlackRock's Aladdin

BlackRock, one of the world's largest asset management firms, utilizes its AI-driven platform, Aladdin, to enhance portfolio management and risk assessment. Aladdin combines machine learning, big data analytics, and predictive modeling to provide actionable insights and optimize investment strategies.

The platform's AI capabilities enable BlackRock to analyze vast amounts of financial data, assess portfolio risks, and identify investment opportunities with greater accuracy. Aladdin's success demonstrates the significant impact of AI on institutional trading and portfolio management.

How Hedge Funds and Institutions Use AI

Hedge funds and institutional investors are at the forefront of AI adoption in trading, leveraging the technology to gain a competitive advantage and enhance their investment strategies. Here's how these entities are utilizing AI to transform the trading landscape:

Algorithmic Trading:

Hedge funds and institutional investors frequently use AI to develop and implement algorithmic trading strategies. These algorithms are designed to execute trades based on predefined criteria and market conditions, allowing for high-frequency trading and precise execution.

AI-powered algorithms can analyze real-time market data, identify trading signals, and execute trades at high speeds. This capability enables institutional investors to capitalize on short-term market opportunities and maintain a competitive edge in fast-moving markets.

Predictive Analytics and Forecasting:

AI is widely used for predictive analytics and forecasting in the financial industry. Hedge funds and institutions employ machine learning models to analyze historical data, forecast market trends, and make data-driven investment decisions.

Predictive analytics allows these entities to anticipate future market movements, assess potential risks, and optimize their trading strategies. By leveraging AI for forecasting, institutional investors can make more informed decisions and enhance their overall performance.

Risk Management and Optimization:

AI plays a crucial role in risk management for hedge funds and institutional investors. AI systems can analyze complex datasets, assess risk factors, and develop strategies to mitigate potential losses.

AI-driven risk management tools help institutions optimize their portfolios, implement dynamic risk controls, and monitor market conditions in real-time. This approach enables them to adapt to changing risk profiles and protect their investments.

Sentiment Analysis:

Sentiment analysis is an application of AI that involves analyzing news articles, social media posts, and other textual data to gauge market sentiment and investor behavior. Hedge funds and institutions use sentiment analysis to gain insights into market trends and sentiment shifts.

By incorporating sentiment analysis into their trading strategies, institutional investors can better understand market psychology, identify potential market-moving events, and adjust their trading decisions accordingly.

High-Frequency Trading (HFT):

High-frequency trading involves executing a large number of trades at extremely high speeds. AI is integral to HFT strategies, enabling firms to process vast amounts of data, identify trading opportunities, and execute trades within milliseconds.

AI-powered HFT algorithms can analyze market microstructure, detect price discrepancies, and capitalize on short-term arbitrage opportunities. This capability allows hedge funds and institutions to gain a competitive advantage in the HFT space.

Portfolio Management:

AI is increasingly used for portfolio management, helping institutional investors optimize asset allocations, assess portfolio performance, and manage risk. AI-driven portfolio management systems can analyze historical data, evaluate asset correlations, and recommend optimal portfolio adjustments.

By leveraging AI for portfolio management, institutions can enhance diversification, improve risk-adjusted returns, and make data-driven investment decisions.

Fraud Detection and Compliance:

AI is also employed to detect fraudulent activities and ensure regulatory compliance in trading. Machine learning models can analyze trading patterns, identify anomalies, and flag potential instances of fraud or market manipulation. Institutions use AI to enhance their compliance efforts, monitor trading activities, and ensure adherence to regulatory requirements. This application of AI helps maintain market integrity and protect investors.

Customized Investment Strategies:

Hedge funds and institutional investors use AI to develop customized investment strategies tailored to specific objectives and risk profiles. AI algorithms can analyze individual investor preferences, financial goals, and market conditions to create personalized investment solutions.

This approach allows institutions to offer bespoke investment strategies that align with client needs and preferences, enhancing client satisfaction and investment performance.

By leveraging AI, hedge funds and institutional investors are redefining the landscape of trading and investment management. The use of AI in algorithmic trading, predictive analytics, risk management, and other areas provides these entities with advanced tools and insights to achieve superior performance and maintain a competitive advantage. As AI technology continues to advance, its impact on trading and investment practices will likely become even more pronounced, shaping the future of finance.

Chapter Seven

Future Trends in AI and Trading

The intersection of Artificial Intelligence (AI) and trading is a dynamic and rapidly evolving field, with ongoing advancements promising to reshape the financial markets in unprecedented ways. As technology progresses, the role of AI in trading will continue to expand, introducing new methodologies, tools, and strategies. This chapter explores what lies ahead for AI in financial markets, highlighting emerging technologies and trends that will likely influence the future of trading.

What's Next for AI in Financial Markets?

Enhanced Machine Learning Algorithms:

More advanced machine learning algorithms are soon to be developed, which should improve trading decision-making and prediction accuracy. Algorithms will be able to evaluate complicated data, identify complex patterns, and make more informed trading decisions thanks to developments in deep learning, reinforcement learning, and other machine learning approaches.

It is anticipated that new algorithms would enhance the capacity to forecast market moves, maximize trading tactics, and adjust to changing market circumstances. These developments will probably result in AI-driven trading systems that are more accurate and flexible.

Integration of Quantum Computing:

Quantum computing holds the potential to revolutionize AI in trading by significantly increasing computational power. Quantum computers can perform complex calculations at speeds far beyond those of classical computers, enabling the analysis of vast datasets and the modelling of intricate financial systems.

The integration of quantum computing with AI could enhance the capability to solve optimization problems, model market dynamics, and develop advanced trading strategies. As quantum technology matures, its impact on AI-driven trading is expected to be transformative.

Development of Explainable AI (XAI):

Explainable AI (XAI) focuses on making AI systems more transparent and interpretable, allowing users to understand how decisions are made. In trading, XAI can help bridge the gap between complex AI models and human decision-making by providing insights into the rationale behind trading recommendations.

As financial institutions increasingly adopt AI, the demand for explainable models will grow. XAI will facilitate greater trust in AI systems, improve compliance with regulatory requirements, and enhance the overall user experience by making AI-driven decisions more understandable.

Advancements in Natural Language Processing (NLP):

Natural Language Processing (NLP) is set to advance further, enabling AI systems to better understand and interpret textual data such as news articles, financial reports, and social media posts. Enhanced NLP capabilities will improve sentiment analysis, event detection, and market forecasting.

Future NLP advancements will allow AI to extract more nuanced insights from unstructured data, leading to more accurate assessments of market sentiment and better-informed trading decisions.

Rise of Autonomous Trading Systems:

Autonomous trading systems, powered by advanced AI, are

expected to become more prevalent. These systems will operate with minimal human intervention, utilizing AI algorithms to execute trades, manage risk, and optimize portfolios autonomously.

As autonomous trading systems evolve, they will incorporate advanced features such as real-time adaptation to market changes, automated strategy refinement, and self-learning capabilities. The rise of such systems will reshape the landscape of trading, emphasizing the role of AI in fully automated trading environments.

Increased Use of Alternative Data Sources:

The incorporation of alternative data sources, such as satellite imagery, geolocation data, and blockchain analytics, will become more prominent in AI-driven trading. These data sources provide unique insights that traditional financial data may not capture, offering additional context for trading decisions.

AI systems will leverage alternative data to enhance predictive models, identify emerging trends, and gain a competitive edge. The integration of diverse data sources will enrich trading strategies and improve the accuracy of market forecasts.

Advances in Behavioral Finance Analysis:

AI's ability to analyze and predict investor behavior will advance, leading to improved understanding of market psychology and decision-making biases. Behavioral finance analysis using AI will provide insights into how collective behavior influences market dynamics and asset prices.

By incorporating behavioral finance principles into AI models, traders and institutions will be better equipped to anticipate market movements driven by psychological factors and investor sentiment.

Greater Emphasis on Ethical AI and Regulation:

As AI becomes more integral to trading, there will be a heightened focus on ethical considerations and regulatory frameworks. Ensuring that AI systems are fair, transparent, and accountable will be essential to maintaining trust and integrity in financial markets.

Regulatory bodies are likely to implement guidelines and standards for AI in trading, addressing issues such as algorithmic bias, data privacy, and market manipulation. The development of ethical AI practices will be critical to ensuring responsible and sustainable use of AI in financial markets.

Evolution of Hybrid AI-Human Trading Models:

Hybrid trading models that combine AI-driven insights with human expertise will gain traction. These models leverage the strengths of both AI and human judgment, allowing traders to benefit from advanced analytics while applying their domain knowledge and experience.

The integration of AI with human decision-making will enhance trading strategies, improve risk management, and foster collaboration between technology and human intuition.

Enhanced Collaboration Across Financial Ecosystems:

AI in trading will require more cooperation between exchanges, brokers, and technology companies, among other players in the financial ecosystem. AI-driven trading systems will function more efficiently overall and will be more innovative thanks to collaborative efforts that also boost data sharing.

Collaborations between banks and AI tech companies will

result in the creation of new instruments, systems, and approaches that expand the possibilities of artificial intelligence in trading.

To sum up, the trading industry's use of AI is expected to witness substantial progress and revolutionary shifts in the near future. Some of the developments that will influence the next wave of AI-driven trade are explainable AI, quantum computing integration, improved machine learning algorithms, and advances in natural language processing. AI will have a significant impact on the financial markets as it develops, providing traders and institutions with new chances to increase accuracy, productivity, and profitability. Navigating the changing world of artificial intelligence in trading will require embracing these future trends and keeping up with technological advancements.

Conclusion

Artificial Intelligence (AI) has enormous and far-reaching potential to revolutionize trade and fundamentally alter the financial markets. As this book has shown, artificial intelligence (AI) is not just a technical development but also a driving force behind a fundamental change in the way that trading is done. Artificial intelligence (AI) is changing every aspect of trading and investing, from improving predictive analytics and trading strategy optimization to transforming risk management and spurring innovation.

This book's journey has shown the amazing ways artificial intelligence is already changing the world. We started by looking at the theories behind artificial intelligence (AI) and machine learning, as well as how these technologies are fundamentally changing the trading sector. We looked at many AI-driven trading platforms and explained how advanced tactics are posted and utilized on them. We demonstrated the tangible benefits that top companies and traders have experienced since incorporating AI into their operations using case studies from real-world business environments. We also looked at risk management, demonstrating how AI technologies could improve stop-loss and take-profit plans to protect capital and maximize profits.

Looking ahead, fascinating developments and new trends will define the use of AI in trading. Better machine learning algorithms will keep pushing the limits of decision-making and prediction accuracy. The ability to process and analyze complicated financial data will be revolutionized by the integration of quantum computing, which promises to give hitherto unheard-of processing power. Explainable AI will increase openness and confidence, facilitating a better understanding and practical application of AI systems. Natural language processing advances will help us better grasp market emotions and happenings and give traders access to even more sophisticated analytical tools.

Hybrid models, which strike a balance between the analytical power of AI and the human traders' intuitive judgment, are anticipated to become more and more popular. They do this by fusing AI-driven insights with human expertise. Through this integration, trading techniques, risk management, and a cooperative approach that capitalizes on the advantages of both AI and human decision-making will all be improved. Future financial ecosystems will also work together more, with partnerships between internet companies and financial institutions fostering innovation and enhancing data exchange. The potential and influence of AI in trading will be further enhanced by these partnerships, which will result in the creation of new tools and platforms.

In conclusion, the development of AI in trading is a current revolution that is drastically changing the market, not some far-off dream. With AI's continued development, traders and institutions will have more chances to increase accuracy, productivity, and profitability. To successfully navigate the future of trading, one must embrace the possibilities of AI and stay educated about these advances. Traders may take the lead in this exciting transformation by recognizing and utilizing AI's transformative capacity, which will allow them to reap its benefits and spur more innovation in the financial markets.

The End!!!

Got Value From This Book? Please Remember To Leave an Honest Review After You Order. Also Check Out other books by Nathan G. Carter on Amazon.

Nathan G. Carter
Thanks.

16073158R00049